anian
£3.99

Original Sylvanian Families™

Edited and compiled by Michael Stuart Phipps
Activity artwork by Paul Gamble
All other artwork by Mario Capaldi
Cover painted by John Burns

A Question Of Curiosity

This is Sylvania . a place where dreams have a wonderful habit of coming true.

SHH!

One day Grover had been studying the sky with particular curiosity. There were so many things about it he didn't understand.
It seemed so big and blue and far away. Grover wondered what it would feel like to touch it.
Grover went to ask his Father,but Durwood was very busy in his workshop, and had no time to answer questions about the sky .
Go and ask your mother.
Grover went to ask his Mother, but Pansy was already in the middle of a muddle with the laundry. She also had no time to spare.
You should ask your teacher, Grover.
Pansy told Grover to ask Aristotle Treefellow at school the next day. Grover thought that this was a very good idea.

The next day Aristotle was in the middle of a maths lesson, and Grover couldn't have chosen a worse time to ask his question.

Grover stood up in the middle of the class. "Yes sir," he said, "I have a question. What does the sky feel like to touch?"

Aristotle was rather cross with Grover for not paying enough attention to the maths. What did the sky have to do with adding and subtracting?

Maths was all very interesting thought Grover, but he had other interests as well. He still wanted to know about the sky.

As Grover was walking sadly home that afternoon, he met Ernest Evergreen, who was always friendly and cheerful.

Grover liked Ernest. He was always inventing interesting things. He decided to ask him his question. He was sure that Ernest could help.

Ernest smiled. "That's a very interesting question," he said. "Perhaps my latest invention will be able to help us find out?"

"Can you sew, Grover?" asked Ernest. "No," said Grover. "Then I shall teach you," said the inventor. "Soon my invention will be ready!"

Ernest brought Grover a needle and cotton and showed him how to sew together the huge pieces of cloth he needed.

They worked hard all afternoon and even Logan Evergreen helped. Soon Ernest's invention was ready and Grover was getting very excited.

They had been working on a big, hot air balloon. Ernest promised to take both Grover and Logan up in it.

The fire warmed the air inside the balloon and it slowly began to rise up. Then Grover climbed into the basket with the other two.

Ernest controlled the fire. The balloon floated higher and higher, above the Sylvanian forest and into the deep, blue sky.

It was a lovely feeling being up in the sky. Grover smiled and Ernest smiled back at him. "Does that answer your question?" he asked.

"Oh yes," said Grover. It definitely did. There was really nothing quite like it. It was simply wonderful!

SPOT THE DIFFERENCE

There are ten differences between the picture below and that on the opposite page. Can you spot them all?

Muddy McBurrows is now playing a trombone instead of a clarinet. Birch Timbertop has changed to Barnaby Oakwood. Bubba Babblebrook has now got orange spots on his trousers. Misty Waters has changed into Roger Waters. Grover Chestnut is now playing a guitar instead of a banjo. The dandelion had changed into a rose. The apples have changed into pears and bananas. A butterfly and a fence have suddenly appeared.

When it's cold and wet outside, Breezy and Bubba Babblebrook can be found sitting by the fireside waiting for their Grandfather Cliff Babblebrook to tell them a story. . .

It's A Quiet Life!

Once Upon a Time. . .

Flora is the quietest member of the Wildwood family. Herb and Ginger love to throw parties. They like to sing and dance and make merry, but not Flora. Rusty and Hollie both enjoy parties, and Smokey may be old, but he loves anything the children like. Flora is just the odd one out. She likes to lead a quiet life.

It's not that Flora doesn't want the others to have fun. On the contrary, whatever makes them happy, makes her happy too. It's just that, if it was up to her, they need never have any parties. Flora prefers things to be nice and quiet. She enjoys them like that.

"You know," she would often say to the children, if their games became too noisy, "peace and quiet are two of my favourite things." Then she would smile her loving smile, and Rusty and Hollie would understand. They did try to keep the noise down, it was just that sometimes they were too excited, and they would forget.

Flora liked to rock in her rocking chair, and think about things. If there wasn't a baby about, then she might knit stockings or sew something. She liked to put on her reading glasses and read a good book. She liked a lot of things, but all of them were quiet.

Herb was planning a party. He loved to invite all his friends round to have a good time. He was very popular, so when all his friends were there, the house was packed. Ginger was helping him to work out all the details.

"We'll have to have plenty of food and delicious fruit punch," she said.

"Of course," agreed Herb. "I've written out a guest list and it's rather long."

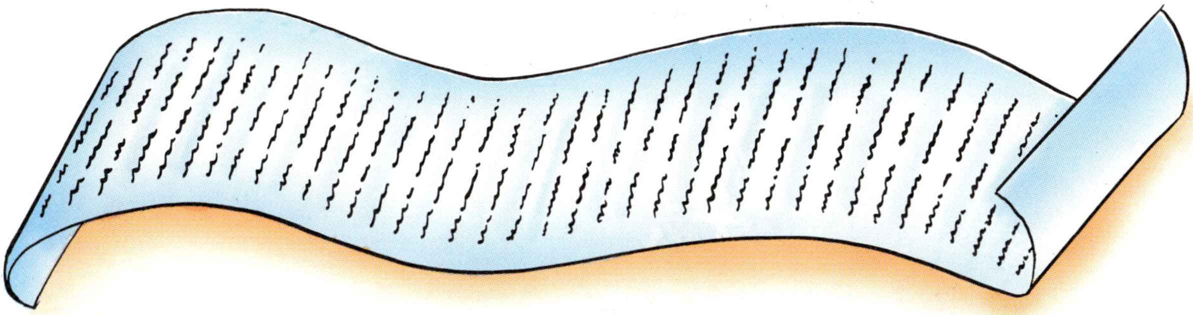

Flora was listening to the conversation and she sighed a quiet sigh. She could see the list from where she was sitting and it certainly was long! Why there must have been forty names on it. That would mean a lot of noise, especially if . . .

"Rusty can play some music for us," suggested Ginger, "We can get everybody to sing songs."

"Oh dear," thought Flora. "Just as I suspected it's going to be noisy."

"How does next Friday sound to you?" asked Herb.

"Not good at all," thought Flora.

"Great," said Ginger. "If it's a nice evening we can have the party outside."

"Maybe it will rain," thought Flora, but she didn't say anything. She knew that everyone else was going to enjoy the party. She didn't want to be the one to spoil their fun.

Friday came along and the party preparations were well under way. It wasn't a birthday party or a holiday party – and it wasn't a wedding party either. It was just a party for the sake of a party.

Flora had tried to find an excuse to get away. She was not against the party, but she would rather have spent the evening quietly.

When the evening came it was anything but quiet. The house and garden were soon full of all the Wildwoods' friends. The Slydales, the Oakwoods, the Timbertops, the Evergreens . . . In fact every family in Sylvania was there. They were chatting and drinking fruit punch, and what a noise they made together!

Then Rusty began to play some music on his tambourine. Everyone danced and sang familiar songs. It was even noisier now, and Flora found it hard to bear. The singing was so loud.

Now, Herb and Ginger had two babies, Juniper and Barkley. Juniper was an easy-going baby. She could sleep through a hurricane, so the party was no problem for her. She was sound asleep.

Barkley, on the other hand, would never sleep when there was a party going on. He would hum along to the music instead. The only problem was the next day he would be tired and cranky. All he would be able to do was cry.

Barkley was awake. Flora went to check on him and found him humming in his bed.

"I could get him back to sleep," suggested Flora, "if I took him over to the Evergreens' house. It's quiet there, and he'd soon fall back to sleep again."

"That's okay with me," said Primrose Evergreen.

"But Flora," protested Ginger. "That means that you will miss the lovely party."

"I'll be all right," said Flora. "Barkley needs the sleep."

So Flora took baby Barkley over to the Evergreens' house. She rocked in Primrose's rocking chair with Barkley on her lap and she sang him soft lullabies. Soon Barkley had fallen fast asleep, and Flora was happy too.

"This is the kind of party I like," she thought. "A nice quiet party, just for two!" **THE END**

Preston Evergreens
SYVANIAN FAMILY FUNNIES

Ernest Evergreen was strolling through the woods with Logan. As Logan glanced up he saw a winged sycamore tree seed spinning through the air as it fell. "Oh, look! It looks like a helicopter. Could you make a helicopter for me Ernest?" begged Logan.
"Well, I could show you how to make a paper helicopter" replied Ernest.

MAKE A HELICOPTER

Follow Ernest's simple instructions if you would like to make a helicopter. You will need:

a 30 centimetres ruler, a pair of round ended scissors, a piece of thick paper, sellotape and a small piece of blu-tack or plasticine.

1. Draw a rectangle shape which measures 25 centimetres long by 11 centimetres wide on your paper, then cut it out.

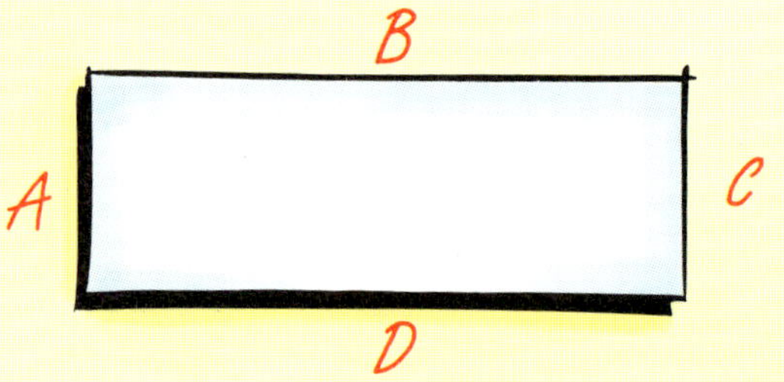

2. Draw a central line through the length of the rectangle from side A to C. From side A measure and cut 16 centimetres along this line.

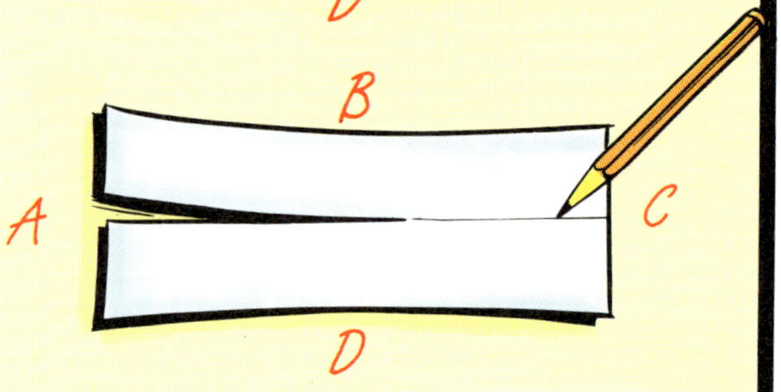

3. From side C measure 5 centimetres along the line. At this point draw a vertical line from side B to D.

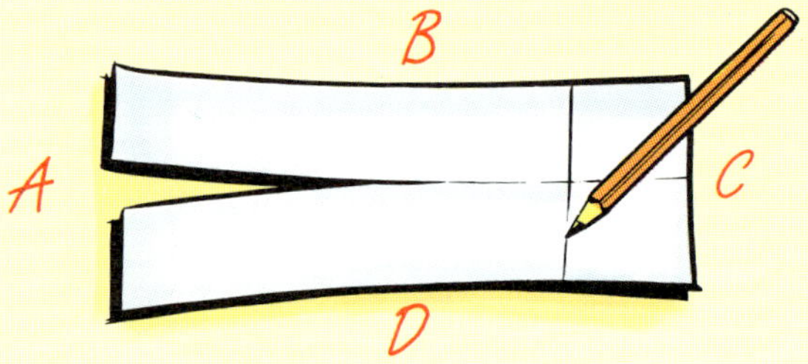

4. From side B cut this vertical line 2 centimetres towards the centre and do the same from side D. (see diagram)

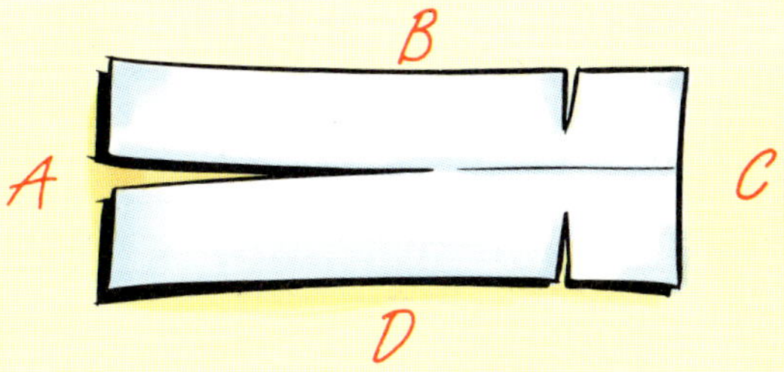

5. Fold the paper as shown in the diagram.

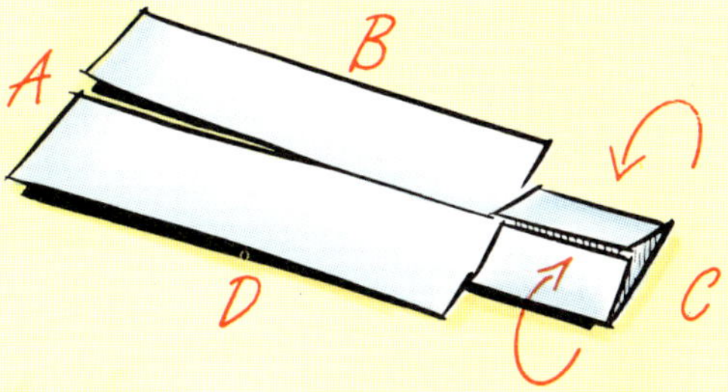

6. Place a small piece of blu-tack (or plasticine) under the fold for weight.) Seal the fold neatly with sellotape.

7. Hold the paper as in the diagram. Gently fold one blade towards you and one blade away from you.

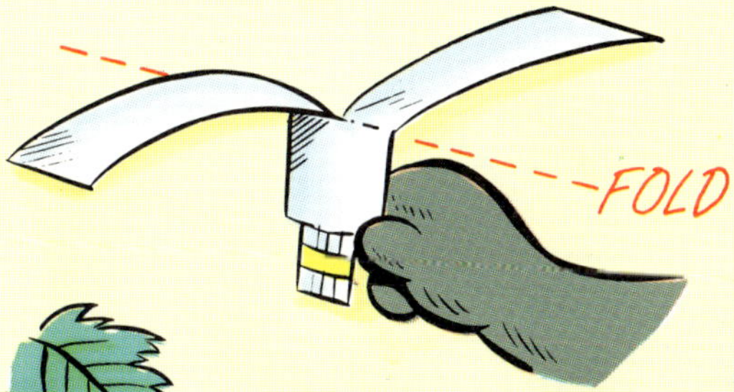

8. Now for the **TEST FLIGHT!** Hold your model high (as in fig. 7) and release it. It should spin to the ground, just like a helicopter.

HELPFUL HINTS

If the helicopter falls too qucikly reduce the weight of the blu-tack. Try different weight papers and length of blades to see if you can improve its flight.

MEMORY TEST

Aristotle asks his pupils to look at the drawings on the blackboard for 30 seconds. The pupils then write down the items they remember. How many can you remember?

Original Sylvanian Families
A Job For Breezy
This is Sylvania, where work can be a pleasure not a chore!
Rocky Babblebrook runs the Sylvanian general store. His little shop stocks just about every single thing you could ever want to buy.
What would you like?
Breezy Babblebrook loves her Father's shop. It's full of lots of lovely things. Sometimes she comes into the shop just to look at everything.

Her Father doesn't mind, as long as she is good. Usually, if Breezy asks her Dad for something, he will let her have it!
As long as it is something small, like a fresh crispy apple, or a little spinning top or a little bag of brown nuts.
Please can I have an apple?
But one day Breezy's eyes fell upon something a little bigger. She stopped in her tracks, opened her mouth and stared.
She was looking at the most beautiful shiny pair of roller skates she had ever seen. They were hanging up high in the big shop window.
Breezy asked her Dad if she could have them but he shook his head. He said they were far too expensive.

Now, Breezy Babblebrook always likes to have her own way, so she protested very strongly. She wrinkled her nose and stamped her foot.

She whined and grizzled and grizzled and whined, but still her Dad said "no". He wouldn't just give them to her.

At last he turned to her and scratched his chin. "If you want those roller skates," said Rocky, "You will have to earn them."

"You can work here in the store with me," said Rocky. "On Saturdays or after school." Breezy wasn't so sure about the idea!

But she did really want those shiny red skates. She looked at them hanging in the window, and decided to give it a try.

Breezy set to work, and after a while she found that she liked working in the store, and meeting all the customers.
Hello, Mrs. Thistlethorn.
She tidied the shelves, sorted out the till, swept the floor and helped to keep the stock up in the shop.
Then she swept the floor again and dusted the counter. She cleaned the windows and polished the door knob. She brushed away cobwebs too!
Sometimes she even helped to serve the customers. She learnt how to take the money and to give the right change.
Can I get you anything, Mr. McBurrows?
Before very long her Father decided she had worked hard enough for the roller skates which she had wanted.

He smiled, patted her on the back and then he climbed up on the step ladder to fetch them down for her.

But Breezy didn't seem too excited when he gave them to her. "No thanks, Dad," she said, "I'm saving up for something else now!"

Breezy led her Dad across the store. She stopped by the window and pointed to a big, red, shiny bicycle.

Breezy wondered if her Dad would let her carry on working in the store until she could have the bicycle. He smiled at her.

"If you really want that big, red bicycle," said Rocky, "you'll be working here for quite some time, won't you?"

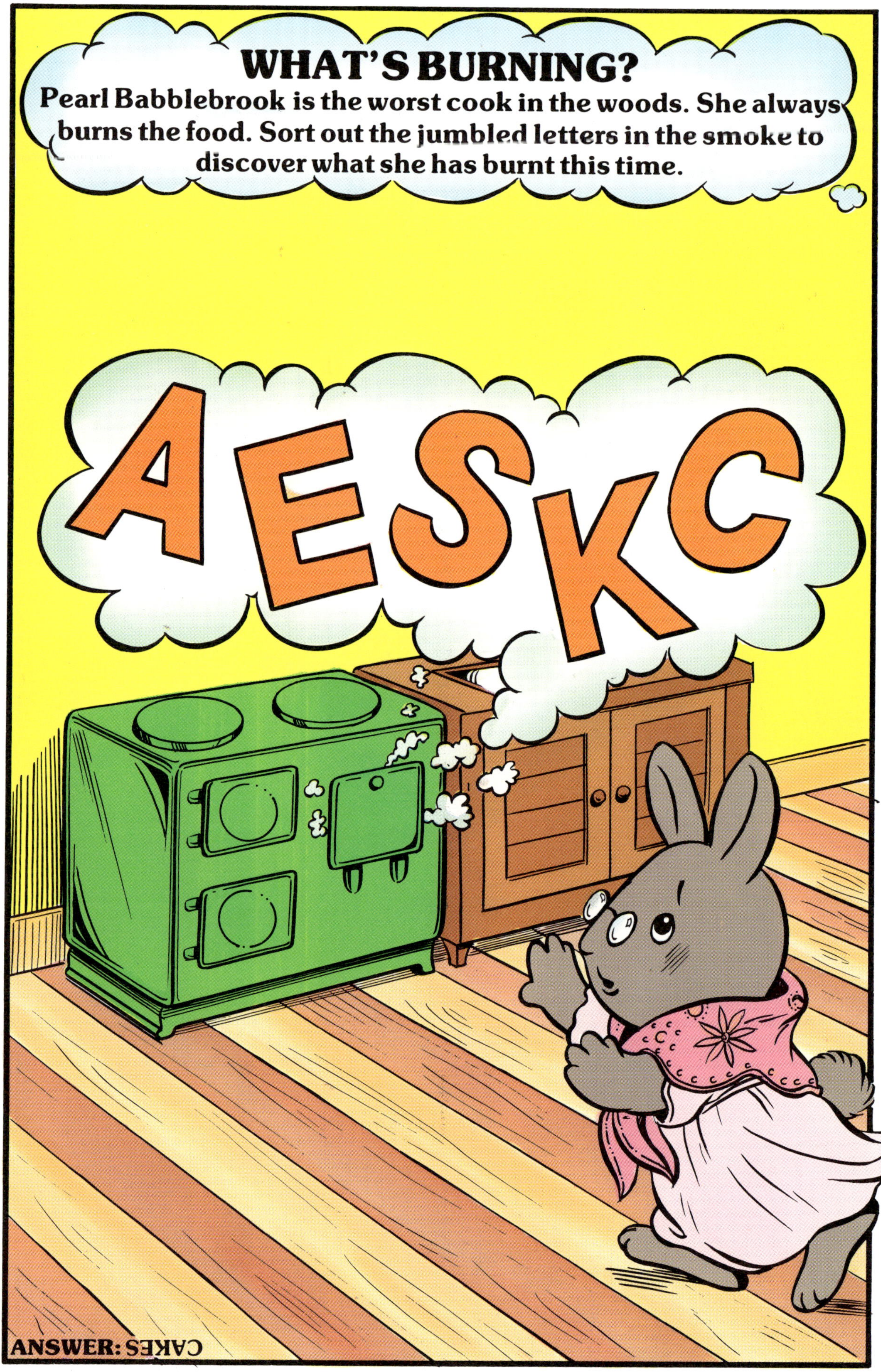
WHAT'S BURNING?
Pearl Babblebrook is the worst cook in the woods. She always burns the food. Sort out the jumbled letters in the smoke to discover what she has burnt this time.
A E S K C
ANSWER: CAKES

WHAT'S COOKING?

Fern Timbertop is a very good cook. Sort out the jumbled letters in the steam from the pan to see what she is boiling.

ANSWER: EGGS

P. GAMBLE.

SYLVANIAN NAME GAME

Complete the names of the Sylvanian characters by writing in the box the first letter of the objects above that box.

G	u	s

TIMBERTOP

VELVETTE

S	L	b	d	A	L	e

p	A	p	s	b

CHESTNUT

WADE

W	a	t	e	R	s

When it's cold and wet outside, Breezy and Bubba Babblebrook can be found sitting by the fireside waiting for their Grandfather Cliff Babblebrook to tell them a story. . .

Mo McBurrows Goes Missing

Once Upon a Time. . .

Digger McBurrows was working. He'd been asked to help make a tunnel somewhere. Heidi wanted to go out into the garden for a little while. She was planting some geraniums. That was why Molly and Muddy were sort of babysitting.

Molly and Muddy were not really used to babysitting. It was a big responsibility and they were both sure that they weren't ready for it. Besides, it meant they couldn't go out to play, and what if something happened while they were in charge?

"Nothing is going to happen," said Heidi. "I'm sure you will be able to handle those two, and you can come and fetch me in the garden, if you need to. It will give you both a chance to get to know your baby Brother and baby Sister better."

Molly and Muddy looked at Monty and Mo crawling about on the floor. Their faces were covered with mush from the apples they had been eating. Molly and Muddy wondered if they really did want to get to know them better.

"Were we really like that too?" asked Molly.

"What do you mean?" asked Heidi. "So small?"

"No," said Molly. "I mean so messy!"

"You still are!" laughed Heidi. "Some of you more than others."

Muddy hung his head. "Thanks a lot, Molly," he thought. "I'll probably have to go and wash my hands again, now!"

But he didn't. Heidi picked up her gardening gloves and her trowel, and went out into the garden.

Molly and Muddy were surprised to find they had a lot of fun, playing on the floor with Monty and Mo. Except Monty and Mo didn't really know how to play, so they just had to keep showing them. Then as soon as they saw how to do something like peek-a-boo, they just kept wanting to do it again and again and again.

After a while, Molly and Muddy were getting tired of all this and Monty and Mo were tired too.

"I think it's time for you to have a nap," said Muddy to Monty, feeling very grown-up.

"Time for you too," said Molly to Mo.

They carried the two babies upstairs and put them into their cots. Mo went straight to sleep, snuggling up in her blankets, but Monty kept wriggling about. He wriggled so much that his blanket would fall out on the floor!

Muddy kept picking up the blanket to put it back over him, but every time he did so, Monty cried some more. Anyway, he always kicked it out again, so Daisy suggested they leave it on the floor until he fell asleep.

"Babies are funny," thought Muddy.

After about fifteen minutes, Muddy and Molly went back to check on Monty and Mo. Monty was sound asleep, but Mo was. . . GONE!

"She must have climbed out over the side of the cot!" cried Molly.

"She couldn't have gone very far!" said Muddy.

They began to search the house. They looked high and low, in every nook and cranny, even under the wardrobes and in the bread bin, but Mo was nowhere to be seen! They started again and looked everywhere they had looked before and some other places that they never thought of, like under the sink and inside the toy chest, but there was no Mo!

"She couldn't have gone out," said Muddy.

"Where is she then?" asked Molly.

"She must have gone out!" said Muddy.

Muddy searched all through the garden, under the hedges and inside the bushes, but he didn't find Mo. Heidi watched him, but she guessed he must just be playing one of his games.

"Children are funny," she thought.

While Muddy was looking outside, Molly was inside searching the house for a third time. How could they lose their baby Sister? What would their Mother think? Clunk. It was the front door. They were about to find out.

Muddy had run to the back door when he saw his Mother going inside. Molly let him in.

"She's come in," said Molly.

"I know," said Muddy. "What are we going to do?"

"I suppose we'd better just tell her," said Molly.

"Tell her what?" asked Heidi. She had just walked into the room.

"It's about Mo," said Muddy.

"What about Mo?" asked Heidi. "I just looked in on her and she's fast asleep."

"She is?!" asked Molly. "How did she get back in her crib?! We thought she was lost!"

"She had just snuggled down under the covers," laughed Heidi. "You must not have seen her! She always does that!"

"She does?" asked Muddy.

"She does," said Heidi. "And I can see I'm going to have to let you two babysit more often!"

THE END

What is grey with big ears and has a trunk?
Rocky Babblebrook going on holiday!
Chester – I'm so hungry I could eat a horse!
MEEOW!
Preston Evergreens
SYVANIAN FAMILY FUNNIES
Birch – How do you stop a mole digging in your garden?
HEE HEE!
Myrtle – You have to hide his spade!
Aristotle – I hope I did not see you cheating!
EXAM
Prissy – So do I!

MOLLY'S PICTURE BOX STORY

Cliff Babblebrook tells the tallest tales you've ever heard. Little Molly McBurrows can't tell stories as well as Cliff, so she decided to make a picture box story which would help her stories be as entertaining as Cliff's. If you would like to make one then why not do as Molly did.

1. First of all Molly gathered together a large cardboard box, two long tubes, (eg from kitchen foil or kitchen towel,) some coloured pencils, paints or crayons, some sticky tape, some paper to draw on and a pair of scissors.

2. Then Molly cut a large rectangular hole in the front of the box.

3. She then cut out two holes from both sides of the box as shown in the diagram opposite. The holes are big enough to slide the two long cardboard tubes through both sides of the box.

4. Molly then drew four or five very simple pictures on the paper, (this must be slightly smaller than the size of the box.) Her pictures told a funny story about Muddy, her Brother. Why not create your own story or maybe draw your favourite fairy tale?

5. Molly then stuck her pictures together vertically on a long piece of paper and in the correct order. She stuck the top end of the picture strip to the top cardboard tube, then she stuck the bottom end of the strip to the bottom tube.

6. Molly placed the tubes and the pictures back in the cardboard box which she had coloured. As she turned the top tube the pictures moved upwards. Each new picture revealed another part of the story.

A NASTY SURPRISE!

Who is about to receive a nasty surprise from Buster Slydale's toy hairy spider? Follow the paths to find out!

ANSWER: NANCY WATERS

Original Sylvanian Families
Blinky Learns A Lesson
This is Sylvania, a place where there are lots of good things to be found.
Fern Timbertop is famous for her Granberry pie.
Hello, Gran.
The recipe is a secret, but everyone knows that Fern uses berries from the forest.
Will you bake us a Granberry Pie?

SHH!
One day, Fern agreed to bake a Granberry pie for Ivy and her friends.
They all had to go out into the forest and collect the berries for the pie though.
You'll each need to take a basket.
Blinky Treefellow didn't want to go picking berries. He was too busy sitting and thinking.
Do I have to?
Fern told Blinky that if he wanted a share of the pie, he would have to share picking the berries as well.
Off you go now!
So Blinky went off with the others to the forest.

When they reached the berry patch, Blinky just sat down again with his thoughts.

Blinky may be very good at thinking, but he's not very good at working!

While the others were busy filling their baskets with the berries, Blinky was sitting so quietly that he fell asleep.

Soon Ivy and the others were ready to go back. Their baskets were full to the brim with lovely berries.

Blinky's basket was still empty. When Bubba Babblebrook woke him up, Blinky began to be worried.

Blinky wanted some pie, but most of the berries had already been picked. He could only find a couple nearby.

He quickly put them into his basket and hurried off. "The others have picked enough for all of us," he thought.

But later, when Fern served up her Granberry pie, Blinky was in for a sorry surprise.

On Blinky's plate there was just a tiny two berry piece of pie.

Blinky knew he had only picked a couple of berries, but now he felt sad and sorry.

Ivy and the others felt sorry for Blinky too, when they saw him looking so glum. Fern gave them a knowing wink.

They all offered Blinky a share of the berries they had picked themselves.

Blinky thanked them very much as Fern served him up a big delicious slice of pie.

Blinky still likes to sit and think, but he also likes Granberry pie.

Now whenever he thinks about that day with the berries, he knows he learned a little about helping out and friends.

When it's cold and wet outside, Breezy and Bubba Babblebrook can be found sitting by the fireside waiting for their Grandfather Cliff Babblebrook to tell them a story. . .

Ivy Timbertop Saves The Day

Once Upon a Time. . .

Ivy Timbertop was so excited! Woody Honeypot was going to marry Hazel and Ivy was going to be a bridesmaid. It was the best thing that Ivy could imagine in the whole world.

It was to be a big wedding. Everybody in Sylvania would be there. There were so many things to arrange and prepare. Hazel was very busy with it all.

Ivy felt as if she was the one getting married. There seemed to be butterflies flapping about in her stomach whenever she thought about it. She wanted to do whatever she could to help Hazel get ready.

"Perhaps I could help you with the sewing," suggested Ivy, when she called on Hazel one afternoon. "I love to sew, you know, and I'm quite good at it. My dad still wears the very first shirt I ever made him."

"I know," said Hazel,"but . . ."

"There must be a lot of sewing to make your wedding dress," continued Ivy. "I'll bet there are yards and yards of pretty material. You'll have to get started soon if it's going to be ready in time!"

"That's just it," said Hazel. "I have already started. I was fitted for my dress last month by a professional seamstress. I expect the dress to be finished the day after tomorrow."

Ivy was rather disappointed. She would have loved to work on Hazel's wedding dress. When it arrived however, she could understand why Hazel didn't ask her to make it.

It was the most beautiful dress that Ivy had ever seen. There were indeed yards and yards of material, but the way it was sewn together was not as simple as Ivy had imagined. Even Ivy didn't think she could have made something like that!

Nevertheless, Ivy still wanted to make herself useful, and as sewing was what she was best at, sewing was what she thought she should offer.

"What about the bridesmaids' dresses?" Ivy asked Hazel. "There's Prissy Thistlethorn and Hollie Wildwood as well as me. That's three dresses and that's a lot of sewing, isn't it?"

"Yes," said Hazel, "but ..."

"Maybe we could wear flowery material," continued Ivy. "Or maybe pink with purple bows. You'll have to decide soon you know."

"Yes," said Hazel. "I already have decided, Ivy. The same seamstress who made my dress is making your dresses as well."

Ivy was very happy when she saw the bridesmaids' dresses. They were almost as lovely as Hazel's wedding dress and they fitted perfectly, but she still wished that there was something she could do to help.

"I understand," said Rose, when Ivy talked to her about it. "But Hazel does seem to have everything under control, and it is her wedding."

"I know," said Ivy sadly.

"Perhaps what you should do is make a wedding present," suggested Rose. "You could use you sewing skills to make them something very special, I'm sure."

It was a good suggestion and soon Ivy had a fine idea of what to make for Hazel and Woody.

When the day of the wedding finally arrived, Ivy hadn't quite managed to finish her wedding present. She had brought it to the church in a little bag. If she could find a few moments she would finish it later on.

Prissy and Hollie were waiting outside with Ivy for the bride to arrive. She was late, as was the custom, but when she arrived she looked more beautiful than anyone had ever seen her.

Then it happened! Disaster struck! As Hazel was walking through the church garden, her lovely long wedding dress blew in a little breeze and caught upon a thorny rose! The dress was torn!

Hazel began to cry. "It's ruined! It's ruined! What will I do?!"

Quick as a flash Ivy ran to get her sewing bag. She brought a needle and some fine white cotton and began to repair Hazel's wedding dress. It only took her a few moments, and her stitches were so careful and so fine that not a trace of the tear could be seen at all.

Hazel wiped her tears away, and smiled at Ivy. She began to cry again, but only because she was so happy!

The wedding went according to plan after that, and it was truly wonderful. Before the reception, Ivy managed to find a moment to sew the last few stitches on her present.

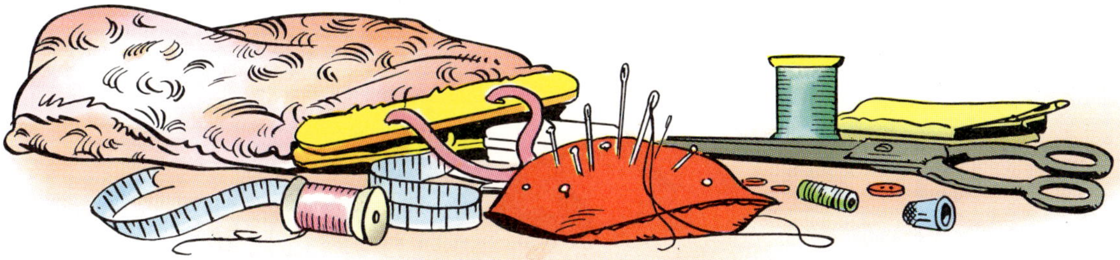

"I'll never be able to thank you enough for your fantastic repair of my dress," said Hazel. "I never realised just how clever you were with a needle."

"Then I hope you will like this as well," said Ivy, handing her her present. It was an embroidery which read HOME SWEET HOME, and that's where the Honeypots put it; over the mantlepiece in the sitting room of their happy newlywed home! **THE END**

CHESTER'S PICTURE CROSSWORD

Chester Thistlethorn is the editor of the Sylvanian newspaper. On the children's page he often prints a picture crossword puzzle.

Using the pictures as clues, see if you can fill in this puzzle.

PAPER DANCERS

Molly McBurrows is clever with her hands and entertains herself and her family with things she makes. One of her party tricks is making paper dancers.

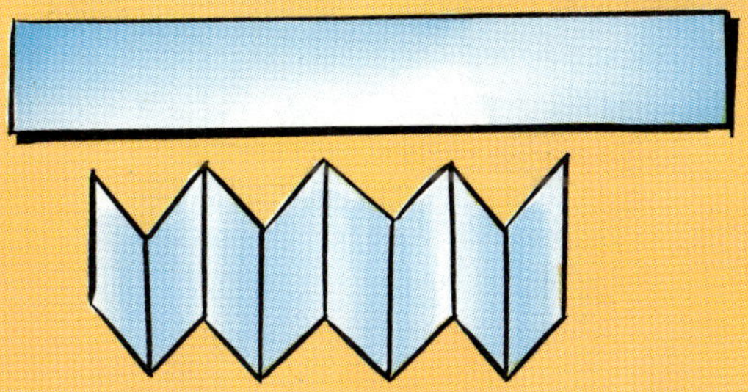

1. Make even sized folds on a long strip of paper, (or newspaper) to resemble the diagram opposite.

2. Press the folds together like a concertina until it is as flat as possible.

3. Draw the shape of a body on the top fold of paper. Make sure you draw right up the paper's edge.

4. Cut out the shaded areas around the body, (see diagram)

5. Open out the folds and there you are! Paper dancers. If you would like the dancers to stand up by themselves, tape two end dancers together to form a circle.

Why not try different shaped dancers; it could be fun!

SMOKEY'S SPECTACLE SEARCH

When Smokey Wildwood takes off his spectacles he always loses them. For this reason he keeps eight pairs! Help Smokey to find all his spectacles hidden in the picture.

A RUSTY REPEAT

Which two pictures of Rusty Wildwood are identical?

ANSWER: 1 and 5

When it's cold and wet outside, Breezy and Bubba Babblebrook can be found sitting by the fireside waiting for their Grand father Cliff Babblebrook to tell them a story. . .

Preston Evergreen The Joker

Once Upon a Time. . .

Preston Evergreen is a joker. He's always trying to be funny, especially in school. He fools about in class the whole time!

Luckily for Preston he really can be very funny indeed. Sometimes even the teacher laughs at his jokes and he is very popular with the other children.

One time, Preston brought in an apple for the teacher. Now most children would have put it on the teacher's desk, but not Preston. He put it on the teacher's chair instead!

It was a very, very ripe apple, and Mrs Treefellow didn't see it when she came in. She sat down with a big SQUASH! That was not one of the times the teacher laughed, though some of the other children couldn't help giggling!

The truth of the matter was that everyone was used to Preston's jokes and jests. They almost expected them. Or at least they expected that they never knew what to expect with Preston.

The big problem was that with all his fooling around, Preston tended to miss what the teacher was teaching. Sometimes Preston would fall behind in his lesson. It wasn't that he was stupid, it was just that he spent so much time being silly.

This never bothered Preston too much, and he always managed to catch up again on his lesson, but then one day. . .

Arabella Treefellow was teaching a class on identifying trees. This was a very useful thing to know. She showed the children the shapes of different types of leaves and explained how they could tell which trees they came from. It wasn't that difficult to learn.

It was not unusual, but Preston wasn't listening to all of this. He was too busy making funny faces at Prissy Thistlethorn to see if he could get her to giggle. So when Mrs Treefellow asked him to identify the oak leaf, Preston was taken by surprise.

Preston looked at the leaf, but he didn't say anything. The leaf looked very familiar, but he couldn't put a name to it.

"Come on, Preston," said Arabella. "Weren't you paying attention?" She knew he hadn't been.

Still Preston said nothing. He didn't know what to say. He began to feel embarrassed.

"Really, Preston!" said Arabella. "This was one of the very first leaves I taught you! If you don't stop fooling about, it will be a wonder if you learn anything at all!"

Arabella hoped to shock Preston into realising that he needed to pay more attention. She didn't realise he was taking it to heart.

"Where's Preston?" asked his Father, Forrest Evergreen, that evening.

"He's up in his room," said Honeysuckle. "He's been up there quietly all evening. I was rather worried about him, but he seems to be doing his homework."

"His homework!" exclaimed Forrest. "Has he turned over a new leaf? Or do you think he could be ill?" Forrest was the local doctor.

There were no jokes at the dinner table that evening, and when he had finished, Preston went straight back to his room.

"I think he *must* be ill," said Forrest. "I'll have to take a look at him."

Preston wasn't ill, but it was the same thing every night that week. No jokes, no laughs, just lots of studying!

Preston was different in school as well. His work was much more consistent, and Arabella was pleased not to have her class interrupted by him. But this was not like Preston. He seemed so sad and serious!

After a week, Arabella had begun to be worried. The other children were too, and no-one was more worried than his Parents Forrest and Honeysuckle. They all missed the lively, happy Preston they used to know, and his cheery sense of humour.

Something had to be done. Not only wasn't Preston joking, but he wasn't smiling either!

Arabella Treefellow had an idea. She went out and found an apple. A very, very ripe apple and she put it on Preston's chair at school.

Now, Preston may have been being very serious, but he was also looking where he was going. So he saw the apple on his chair before he sat on it. He picked the apple up and looked at Mrs Treefellow.

She was looking back at him and she smiled. Preston couldn't help it. He smiled too. Then he started to laugh! He understood.

Preston is still the joker in school. Sometimes he even makes the teacher laugh, but he tries not to let it interfere with his studies.

Arabella has been teaching the children about weights and measures. She knows they need to learn about scales and balance. Preston has learned something about keeping a balance as well! **THE END**

ARISTOTLE'S QUIZ

Aristotle is the headmaster of the Sylvanian school, he often sets a quiz for his pupils. But below he has set a quiz for you about the Sylvanians.

Choose your answer and write a, b or c in each box.

1. WHO CANNOT KEEP HIS CLOTHES CLEAN?

a. Roger Waters
b. Muddy McBurrows
c. Forrest Evergreen

2. WHO LOVES AND COLLECTS HONEY?

a. Molly McBurrows
b. Arabella Treefellow
c. Gus Timbertop

3. WHICH SYLVANIAN IS AN INVENTOR?

a. Prissy Thistlethorn
b. Ernest Evergreen
c. Ollie Oakwood

4. WHO LOVES EXPLORING?

a. Blinky Treefellow
b. Myrtle Chestnut
c. Birch Timbertop

ANSWERS:
1. b
2. c
3. b
4. c

Scarlett's New Doll

This is Sylvania, a very friendly place.

Scarlett carried Hetti with her everywhere she went. She never let her go for a moment, not even when she went to sleep!
Come on, Hetti.
Nobody but Scarlett was allowed to play with Hetti. She always kept her doll out of her friends' reach.
They weren't allowed to hold or touch her. If someone asked to play with Hetti, the answer would always be NO!
No! You can't hold her!
She was Scarlett's doll and Scarlett made the rules. Why should anybody else play with Hetti when she had been given to her and only her?
Everyone told Scarlett that she should share her doll with the other children, she should be generous and good natured with all of her friends.
Just let them take a look at Hetty?

Scarlett wouldn't listen and clutched Hetti tighter and tighter, frightened that someone would snatch her away.

"Sharing is better," said Barnaby Oakwood. "That's what friends are for." The other Sylvanian children were upset by Scarlett's behaviour.

Scarlett didn't care though. Hetti was her doll and she was the only one allowed to play with her. That was the rule.

One bright and sunny day, Scarlett decided to take Hetti out for a walk. The road led to the Waters' House.

Misty Waters was sitting outside, playing with a doll of her own. She looked so happy and seemed to be really enjoying herself.

Scarlett looked over at Misty curiously. She had never seen a doll like that before. She wondered if it was better than Hetti.
The doll was dressed as a ballerina and Scarlett thought it was lovely. Although Scarlett loved Hetti, she would have given anything to own a ballerina doll.
Scarlett walked over to where Misty was playing. She was very interested in Misty's doll and wanted to ask her about it.
Hello, Misty. Where did you get that doll?
She wished that she could hold it and look at it more closely, but was rather afraid to ask Misty if she could do so.
My Dad gave it to me.
Scarlett went over to Misty and plucked up the courage to ask her if she could hold the ballerina doll.
Can I play with her?

Misty didn't mind if Scarlett played with her doll, on the condition that Scarlett let her play with Hetti. After all that was only fair.
Only if you let me play with **your** doll.
Scarlett looked at Hetti and then at Misty's ballerina doll again, and felt a little bit reluctant to part with her lovely Hetti.
Then suddenly she realised the fun they would have if the two of them exchanged dolls, so Scarlett agreed.
What's her name?
Misty and Scarlett played with the two dolls all afternoon. It was great fun and at last Scarlett learnt something about sharing.
Isabel. What's **yours** called?
Hetti.
"Now I can play with two dolls instead of just the one," Scarlett said. "Sharing is great!" Everybody agreed.

Ashley Evergreen and Bubba Babblebrook complained to Ernest that it was too windy to play outside. "That awful wind has spoiled our fun" Ashley sobbed. "But the wind can be lots of fun," replied Ernest, "I'll prove it to you!"

"WE'LL MAKE A WINDMILL!"

To make a windmill with Ernest you will need: a pencil, some thick paper or card, a paper fastener, a pair of scissors and a short length of narrow width doweling or cane.

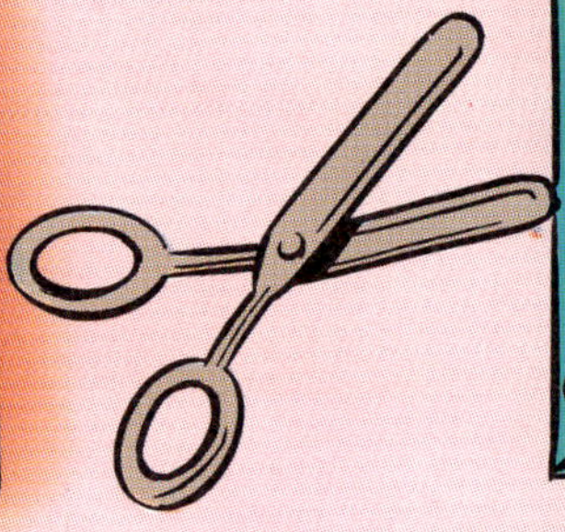

1. First of all divide a small square of paper or card, (approximately 10 centimetres square) into four as in the diagram above. You may like an adult to help you cut along the lines to within 2½ centimetres of the centre.

2. Then very carefully make a hole in the centre large enough for the paper fastener. Then make holes of similar size in the corners as shown in the diagram.

3. Fold the "holed" corners to the centre hole and insert your paper fastener.

4. Attach the legs of the paper fastener to the length of doweling and them make sure the paper can move freely. Then blow on to it and watch your windmill swirl around and around.

MAKE A JIGSAW PUZZLE

Myrtle Chestnut was very upset! She couldn't complete her jigsaw puzzle because some of the places were missing. But Durwood Chestnut made her feel much better. He helped her to make her very own jigsaw puzzle!

Durwood found an old greetings card with a simple picture on the front. Using a pencil and a ruler her divided the front of the card into large equal sized squares. He cut out the squares very carefully with some scissors. Then having jumbled up the squares, he gave Myrtle the pieces of her new jigsaw puzzle to put together again. She was delighted!

1. Find a simple picture. (It doesn't have to be a greetings card.)

2. Divide the picture into large equal squares.

3. Cut out the squares very carefully with the scissors.

Mix up the squares and then sort out your jigsaw puzzle like Myrtle. You may also have hours of fun making jigsaw puzzles from any simple picture such as postcards, magazines and newspaper pictures.

BOO